THE HISPANIC INFLUENCE IN THE UNITED STATES

LATINOS
IN AMERICAN HISTORY

JUNIPERO JOSE
SERRA

BY JIM WHITING

Mitchell Lane
PUBLISHERS

P.O. Box 196
Hockessin, Delaware 19707

THE HISPANIC INFLUENCE IN THE UNITED STATES

LATINOS
IN AMERICAN HISTORY

OTHER TITLES IN THE SERIES

Visit us on the web: www.mitchelllane.com
Comments? email us: mitchelllane@mitchelllane.com

THE HISPANIC INFLUENCE IN THE UNITED STATES

LATINOS
IN AMERICAN HISTORY

JUNIPERO JOSE
SERRA

BY JIM WHITING

Mitchell Lane
PUBLISHERS

Printing   2   3   4   5   6   7   8   9

Library of Congress Cataloging-in-Publication Data

Whiting, Jim, 1943-
    Junípero José Serra / by Jim Whiting.
        p. cm. — (Latinos in American history)
Summary: Traces the life of the Spanish explorer and missionary who travelled to Mexico and California to teach the Indians about Christianity and who established nine missions along the California coast.
Includes bibliographical references (p.) and index.
    ISBN 1-58415-187-0
    1. Serra, Junípero, 1713-1784—Juvenile literature. 2. Explorers—California—Biography—Juvenile literature. 3. Explorers—Spain—Biography—Juvenile literature. 4. Franciscans—California—Biography—Juvenile literature. 5. Franciscans—Missions—California—History—18th century—Juvenile literature. 6. Indians of North America—Missions—California—Juvenile literature. 7. California—History—To 1846—Juvenile literature. [1. Serra, Junípero, 1713-1784. 2. Explorers. 3. Missionaries. 4. California—History—To 1846. 5. Indians of North America—Missions—California.] I. Title. II. Series.
    F864.S44 W485 2003
    979.4'02--dc21

2002014360

ABOUT THE AUTHOR: Jim Whiting has been a journalist, writer, editor, and photographer for more than 20 years. In addition to a lengthy stint as publisher of *Northwest Runner* magazine, Mr. Whiting has contributed articles to the *Seattle Times, Conde Nast Traveler, Newsday,* and *Saturday Evening Post.* He has edited more than 20 titles in the Mitchell Lane Real-Life Reader Biography series and Unlocking the Secrets of Science. He lives in Washington state with his wife and two teenage sons.

PHOTO CREDITS: Cover: Bettmann/Corbis; p. 6 Barbara Marvis; p. 9 Robert Holmes/Corbis; p. 10 Bob Krist/Corbis; p. 14 Hulton/Archive; p. 18 Robert Holmes/Corbis; p. 20 North Wind Picture Archive; p. 22 Bettmann/Corbis; p. 24 Darrell Gulin/Corbis; p. 26 North Wind Picture Archive; p. 28 Monterey County Historical Society; p. 30 James A. Sugar/Corbis; p. 32 Bettmann/Corbis; p. 36 Robert Holmes/Corbis; p. 38 Richard Cummins/Corbis; p. 41 Dave Bartruff/Corbis

PUBLISHER'S NOTE: This story is based on the author's extensive research, which he believes to be accurate.

    The spelling of the names in this book follows the generally accepted usage of modern day. The spelling of Spanish names in English has evolved over time with no consistency. Many names have been anglicized and no longer use the accent marks or any Spanish grammar. Others have retained the Spanish grammar. Hence, we refer to Hernando de Soto as "de Soto," but Francisco Vásquez de Coronado as "Coronado." There are other variances as well. Some sources might spell Vásquez as Vazquez. For the most part, we have adapted the more widely recognized spellings.

CONTENTS

CHAPTER 1

Sleeping Beauty's Castle is one of the main attractions at Disneyland. Millions of vistitors tour the popular Southern California site every year and spend a great deal of money while they are there. This is one of the reasons why California's economy is among the largest in the world.

FACING FAILURE

In 1999 the state of California had the sixth-largest economy in the entire world. It trailed only the United States as a whole, Japan, Germany, France, and the United Kingdom. The value of California's economy was also larger than the combined totals of Spain and Mexico, the two countries that were responsible for its discovery, naming, and early development.

More people lived in California than in any other state in the union, and millions more poured into the state as tourists to lie on its golden beaches, climb its high mountains, sightsee in its great cities, and enjoy the thrilling rides in Disneyland and other theme parks.

To a handful of desperate, starving Spaniards huddled not far from the San Diego shoreline in early 1770, this future prosperity was impossible to conceive. They were the remnants of an expedition of more than 200 men who had arrived there less than a year earlier. To them, what would one day be called the Golden State was a miserable wasteland.

Some had come overland, crossing trackless deserts and rugged mountains. Others had come by sea on sailing ships that frequently covered less than 50 miles a day over often stormy seas. Now many of them were sick. Many others had died, either during the journey or following their arrival. One of San Diego's first landmarks bore a grim name: Puenta de los Muertos, or "Dead Man's Point." It was the burial ground.

The men came from different backgrounds. Some were soldiers. Some were sailors. A few were priests. They all had one thing in common: They were very hungry. Their only food was what they had brought with them the previous year, a supply that was steadily dwindling.

Their only hope was the return of one of the ships that had carried them to San Diego. They had sent it back to Mexico for more supplies and additional men several months earlier. They didn't know if it would ever return. It might have been lost at sea.

Finally their leader made a hard decision. They had been ordered to found a new colony in this vast unknown land. But they had to eat. If they didn't get more food—and get it soon—they would die of starvation.

He set a deadline. If the ship didn't appear by that date, they would have to abandon San Diego, the tiny foothold they had achieved in California. Spain would probably lose its claim to the land. Other countries would move in and take over. California's destiny would be changed forever.

This decision was hard enough for the leader to make. He had been a soldier for almost his entire life. He was accustomed to carrying out the commands of his superiors.

For the priests, the decision was even harder. They believed with all their hearts that their purpose was to convert the local Indian population to the Christian religion. If they departed, they would have failed in that purpose. But they needed the soldiers for protection. They couldn't remain without them.

As each day brought the tiny expedition closer to the ominous deadline, one of the men became especially important.

He was small of stature, standing barely over five feet. He wore the plain gray robe and sandals that identified him as a Franciscan friar. At age 56 he was the oldest and most experienced of the priests.

He had been in the New World for 20 years, spreading the word of the Christian Gospel. For nearly 20 years before that, he had dreamed of serving as a missionary among non-Christian peoples. He viewed this expedition as the high point of his life.

Thousands of souls were waiting on him for their salvation, he believed. It was his duty and his responsibility to go to them.

But every day he looked out over an empty ocean. Every day he saw nothing but an endless series of waves. And every day brought him 24 hours closer to the bitterest disappointment of his life.

His name was Father Junípero Serra, and he needed a miracle.■

This painting of Junípero Serra shows him as a relatively young man. His distinctive haircut is known as a tonsure and is an identifying mark of a priest. The top of his head is shaved, with a fringe of hair encircling his skull.

This is a present-day view of Palma, the capital city of the island of Majorca. Junípero Serra was born in a village on the island in 1713. He moved to Palma in 1729 to begin training to become a priest. He remained in Palma for 20 years before leaving to become a missionary in the New World.

THE
JUNIPER TREE

Miguel José Serra was born in the early morning hours of November 24, 1713, to Antonio and Margarita Serra. As soon as it became light, his parents rushed to their parish church with the newborn. Their first two children had died in infancy, and they wanted to make sure that this youngster was properly baptized in case he too was carried away.

His birthplace was the village of Petra on the Spanish island of Majorca. Majorca is the largest of the Balearic Islands, which lie more than 100 miles east of the Spanish coast in the Mediterranean Sea. Today, the Balearics are a popular tourist destination, especially during the winter months. Thousands of Northern Europeans flock to the islands' sandy beaches to escape freezing temperatures and bask in the sun.

When Miguel was born, most Majorcans lived in villages. Each day they would walk the short distance to their small farms and tend their fields. At an early age young Miguel must have accompanied his parents as they worked the land. They probably grew crops, took care of fruit trees, and looked after a few sheep or cattle.

Religion was very important in their daily lives. The parish church of St. Peter, where the boy was baptized, was on one side of the village. The Franciscan church of San Bernardino was on the other. On a nearby hill was a chapel known as Mare de Déu de Bon Any, "The Mother of God of the Good Year." The inhabitants of Petra and nearby villages made frequent climbs there to worship and pray for success in growing their crops.

Though he was a small, somewhat sickly boy, Miguel would often join them. From the summit he could make out his own house, which is still standing. It is built of stone and has two stories. The living room and kitchen are on the street level. Stairs lead to a large storage area and the bedrooms.

His parents couldn't read or write, but they wanted something better for their son. They enrolled him in the school that was connected with the Franciscan church. Miguel learned how to read and write, add and subtract. He studied Latin and became one of the school's best singers. Every summer he helped his parents with the harvest.

Then, at the age of 15, he made a fateful decision.

He wanted to become a priest.

His parents must have been disappointed. They had only one other child, a girl named Juana María. She had been born three years after Miguel. To give up their one son wasn't easy, but they supported his decision. They made the 25-mile trip to Majorca's capital city of Palma. Miguel began studying at the cathedral there. Soon he decided that he wanted to become a Franciscan friar, or *fray,* as it is known in Spanish.

The Franciscans traced their history back more than 500 years. Francesco di Pietro di Bernardone, born in 1181 in the Italian city of Assisi, was the son of a wealthy merchant. Around 1205 he gave up his worldly goods and began a life of prayer, poverty, and service to the poor. He gathered a small group of followers and founded the Franciscan Order, dedicated to living simply in close harmony with nature. Two years after his death in 1226, he was canonized as St. Francis of Assisi.

Miguel became a novice in the Franciscan Order, which meant that he was on probation while the depth of his religious conviction was tested. He moved into the friary of St. Francis, where he had to perform many menial tasks. There was one task he couldn't perform: He was too short to turn the pages of the large volume of music that the friars and novices sang each day as part of their daily services.

Soon he was considered advanced enough to put on the Franciscan habit. For the rest of his life, he would wear the same clothing. An undergarment of scratchy wool was next to his skin. Over this was a loose-fitting gray robe with a cowl, or hood, and a white cord around his waist. Sandals provided some protection for his feet.

A year later, on September 15, 1731, he made his religious profession. He promised to commit himself to a lifetime of poverty, obedience, and chastity. It was not an easy life, but every year afterward he renewed those same vows.

He had to decide on a new name for himself to symbolize his new life. As one of the closest followers of St. Francis, he chose Junípero, after the sturdy juniper tree. The juniper tree stood firmly no matter how strongly the winds blew.

Even though he was now a full member of the Franciscan Order, he continued his religious studies at the friary. Six years later he became a lecturer of philosophy there. At the age of 24, he was only a few years older than his students. Soon afterward he was ordained as a priest in the Catholic Church.

In 1742 he received his doctorate in philosophy and left the friary to become a professor at the University of Palma. He was a successful and popular teacher, both at the friary and at the university. Two of his students, Francisco Palóu and Juan Crespí, would accompany him in many of his future travels. Palóu would write the first biography about his one-time teacher. The book is one of the main sources for information about Serra himself and the early Spanish missionary activity in California. Crespí would keep a diary of their journeys.

Successful as he was, Serra wasn't satisfied as a university professor. Something was gnawing at him.

When he entered the Franciscan Order, his studies had suggested that his true calling was to preach the Holy Gospel to those ignorant of the Christian religion. He decided to heed that calling and become a missionary.

According to Palóu's book, many years later Serra said, "I have had no other motive but to revive in my soul those intense longings which I have had since my novitiate when I read the lives of the saints. These longings had become deadened because of the preoccupation I had with studies."

The opportunity to follow his heart finally arrived in 1749. A group of missionaries was recruited to serve in Mexico, known at the time as New Spain. Serra was among the first to volunteer.

He was aware that his decision would be difficult for his family. Even though his sister and her husband would inherit the family farm, he knew that leaving would be hard on his parents.

He didn't let them know about his plans until he had arrived in the port city of Cádiz, on the Atlantic Ocean about 25 miles north of the Strait of Gibraltar and more than 400 miles from Majorca. He sent a letter to another Franciscan friar, asking him to break the news to his parents.

"Tell them," he wrote, "how badly I feel at not being able to stay longer and make them happy as I used to do. Nothing else but the love of God has led me to leave them."

At the end of August the ship sailed from Cádiz. Junípero Serra would never see his native land or his family again.■

King Carlos III of Spain (also known as Charles III) made two decisions that had a great impact on Junípero Serra's life. The first was to expel the Jesuits from the missions that they had established in the New World. That enabled Serra and other Franciscan missionaries to take over the missions. The other was to order an expedition into Alta (upper) California to establish Spanish control over the area. Serra became a member of that expedition.

IN NEW SPAIN

T he trip from Cádiz to the island of Puerto Rico lasted seven weeks. Even though Europeans had been making this trip for more than 250 years, it was still not easy. The ship ran low on drinking water because the casks that carried it leaked.

"The shortage of water was our greatest trial," Serra wrote. "I was so thirsty that I would not have hesitated to drink from the dirtiest puddle in the road or anything, no matter what."

The missionaries spent a week in Puerto Rico giving sermons and hearing confessions. Then they set sail for the port city of Veracruz. Almost within sight of land, a storm blew them out to sea again. It wasn't until December 7, 1749, that Serra first set foot in New Spain.

He declined the offer of a horse that could have carried him the 270 miles to Mexico City in relative comfort. Instead, he walked the entire distance, accompanied by one other priest.

The road rose steadily to nearly a mile and a half above sea level. At that time of year it was intolerably hot in his heavy woolen robe during the day and often freezing cold at night. Even worse, at some point in the journey Serra was bitten by a spider or an insect. The wound began to itch unbearably, and as he scratched it he made it much worse. It became swollen and infected. It would bother him for the rest of his life.

Despite the intense pain in his leg, Serra and his companion reached the outskirts of Mexico City on December 31. They arrived at their destination, the Apostolic College of San Fernando, on New Year's Day. The college served several functions: It trained newcomers for their work, provided a place to rest between assignments, and housed retired missionaries until they died.

Serra was so excited and happy about the great work he thought he would perform that he asked permission to take his novitiate all over again, even though he would be with men half his age. While that was denied, he was allowed to pray with the novices each day after doing his regular prayer rounds.

Normally new missionaries were required to spend at least a year at San Fernando, but Serra, Crespí, and Palóu left after five months because of a special opportunity in the Sierra Gorda region. This mountainous area was located 175 miles northwest of Mexico City. Naturally, they walked the entire distance.

Serra, Crespí, and Palóu remained in Sierra Gorda for eight years, establishing missions and overseeing the construction of several graceful churches, which are still in existence. Then they returned to San Fernando, where Serra would spend the next nine years. He was given several responsibilities during that time. One of the most important was conducting "home missions," in which he visited established Christian communities. He would hear confessions, conduct services, and lead other activities to aid their spiritual renewal.

He became well known for his sermons, which he delivered in Mexico City and during his home missions. Sometimes he would treat himself so harshly while he was speaking that his listeners were afraid he might accidentally kill himself. He would hold glowing coals or lighted candles next to his bare skin, whip his back with chains, beat himself on the chest with heavy stones, or wear shirts with sharp wires that lacerated him. It was his way of doing penance for his sins.

Meanwhile, events thousands of miles away were about to unfold and change his destiny.

Following the Protestant Reformation during the 16th century, members of the Society of Jesus, the Jesuits, began to take control of the educational and missionary work of the Catholic Church. In the New World, they established dozens of missions that soon became very prosperous.

As so often happens to a group when it becomes successful, the Jesuits began attracting a number of enemies. Some were jealous. Others were afraid of their steadily growing power. For complicated political reasons, King Carlos III (also known as Charles III) expelled them from Spain in 1767.

The same expulsion order extended to New Spain. The Jesuits were ordered to leave the missions they had founded, often with no more than a few minutes to gather essential belongings. Some had lived there for most of their lives. A few died from the harsh conditions of their departure.

With the Jesuits gone, the Franciscans were given control of the missions. Serra was appointed president of the 14 that were spread out among a 600-mile chain in Baja (lower) California. He gathered a group of his fellow priests that included Palóu and Crespí. Early in 1768, they sailed across the Sea of Cortés, which separates Mexico from Baja California, and assumed their new duties.

Serra began settling into his new responsibilities, believing that he would spend several years in this harsh, sunbaked land.

He was wrong.

Once again, events thousands of miles away that had been set in motion hundreds of years earlier would have a profound influence on his life.■

A statue of Juan Rodríguez Cabrillo. In 1542, Cabrillo led the first Spanish expedition to explore the coast of California. He discovered San Diego and probably sailed as far north as the border with Oregon before storms drove him back. He was badly wounded in a skirmish with Indians when his ships sought shelter and died soon afterward.

THE RUSSIAN THREAT

The Spanish conquistador Hernán Cortés had conquered Mexico City in 1521. He heard rumors of an island that was rich with gold and pearls lying off the western coast of Mexico and went to find it. He believed it was the same island that had been described in a popular book of the time, an island ruled by a queen named Calafia. He called the island California. He tried to settle it but left after barely a year. He could find no gold, the pearls were in several hundred feet of water, Calafia didn't exist, and the land itself was dry and barren.

In 1542 an expedition under the command of Juan Rodríguez Cabrillo sailed up the west coast as far north as the present California-Oregon border. Cabrillo claimed all the land he saw for Spain.

In 1602 Sebastián Vizcaíno (viz-ky-EE-no) sailed along the same coast. He was looking for a safe harbor where Spanish trading galleons from Manila in the Philippine Islands could land and rest up after their long voyage across the Pacific. Before he could find one, his men began dying of scurvy. That is a disease caused by the lack of vitamin C, which is found in fresh fruits. Vizcaíno became desperate. If he continued much longer, there wouldn't be enough men to handle his ship. As soon as he found a large indentation in the coast, he was satisfied. He called it Monterey, wrote that it was a perfect harbor "sheltered from all winds," and returned.

His discovery was soon virtually forgotten.

Captain Gaspar de Portolá was the governor of Baja (lower) California who volunteered to lead the Sacred Expedition. He overcame major difficulties to fulfill his assignment by establishing settlements in San Diego and Monterey.

About 100 years later, Jesuit missionaries pushing north through Mexico turned westward and realized that California was not an island after all. They divided it into two parts: Alta (upper) California and Baja (lower) California. Accompanied by soldiers, the Jesuits turned south into Baja California. They began establishing the string of missions that Serra and the other Franciscans would eventually take over.

The Spaniards left Alta California alone. It was too far away, too hard to get to. It didn't seem to have anything of value.

Several decades passed. Soon after the expulsion of the Jesuits, King Carlos heard some ominous news. Russian fur traders were crossing the Bering Sea to the Aleutian Islands off the coast of Alaska and beginning to sail south from there. Soon they might reach the California coast and establish settlements there. That would give them control of land that the Spanish believed belonged to them.

The Spanish suddenly became interested in Alta California.

They organized what was called the Sacred Expedition. The expedition would begin with the establishment of a mission at San Diego. It would proceed up the coast to Vizcaíno's wondrous harbor of Monterey and establish another one there. Eventually these two original missions—some 400 miles apart—would be connected by a string of additional missions. Each one would be staffed by Franciscan missionaries and guarded by Spanish soldiers. These settlements would cement Spain's control over Alta California and keep out the Russians, or anyone else. In addition, the expedition would bring the Christian religion to the Indian inhabitants of Alta California.

Captain Gaspar de Portolá (gahs-PAR day port-oh-LA), a longtime Spanish soldier and the governor of Baja California, volunteered to lead the expedition.

Junípero Serra was appointed to establish the missions.■

This statue of Father Junípero Serra stands in the garden of Mission San Carlos Borroméo de Carmelo. Founded in 1770, it was the first of the nine California missions that he personally established. He carries a cross in his right hand and cradles a model of a mission in his left hand.

THE SACRED EXPEDITION

The Sacred Expedition would travel both by sea and by land. Three ships would sail from Baja California, while two columns of soldiers would travel overland from Baja California. They would all meet at San Diego. Then Portolá would continue north by land with many of the soldiers to Monterey. One of the ships would sail offshore, carrying supplies for the settlement and mission that they would establish there.

It would not be easy. The northernmost mission in Baja California was still several hundred miles south of San Diego. The men would travel through uncharted territory where there were no roads or trails, driving several hundred head of livestock. The ships would have to travel even farther, sailing around the tip of Baja California and up nearly 1,000 miles of inhospitable shoreline.

One of the ships, the *San Carlos*, departed in January 1769. A month later she was followed by the *San Antonio*. Both ships carried supplies and all the religious materials for establishing the missions. They also carried some soldiers. The third ship, the *San José*, would sail in June.

The first land group departed in March. The second group, which included Portolá and Serra, set out in early May. Even before the departure Serra's leg was so painful that Father Palóu begged him to remain, offering to go in his place.

Serra would have no part of this. Within two days, however, his leg had become so painful that he could barely stand. Portolá urged him to return to the mission. Again Serra refused, so Portolá ordered a litter to be built. It would be carried by several of the Christianized Indians who accompanied the Spaniards. Serra couldn't bear the thought of the poor men carrying him so far and so long. He approached one of the muleteers and asked for help.

"My son, do you know a remedy which might cure my leg?" he asked.

"Father, I know only animals. I am not a surgeon," the man replied.

"Then think of me as an animal," Serra answered.

The muleteer went to work and made a poultice of several herbs. Serra applied it before sleeping, and awoke the next morning almost entirely free of pain. He would use the poultice throughout the journey.

During the long trek Serra encountered truly pagan Indians for the first time. They were naked and, even worse from his standpoint, they didn't show any shame.

Though the expeditions suffered hardships along the way, they arrived in San Diego on July 1. There they encountered a ghastly sight. The *San Antonio* and *San Carlos* had both arrived, but the *San Carlos* had

A view of the church at Mission San Diego de Alcalá. San Diego was the first of the 21 California missions to be established.

taken more than 100 days for the voyage. Most of her crew and some of the soldiers she carried had contracted scurvy, and many had died.

It was clear that neither of the ships could accompany Portolá to Monterey as he had originally planned. Not only would he have fewer men for the land expedition, some of them were ill. Nonetheless his duty was clear. After sending the *San Antonio* on the long voyage back to Mexico for more supplies and additional sailors, he and a group of men departed on July 14 for Monterey. Crespí went with him, and his diary provided many details about what happened during the following months.

Two days after departing, Serra and three other Franciscans founded San Diego de Alcalá. It was the first mission in Alta California. It consisted of a small brush chapel and, later, a slightly larger church made of adobe.

Many of the Spaniards left behind were sick. There wasn't a lot of food, and the local Indians proved reluctant to conversion. One time Serra thought that he was about to perform his first baptism, but the Indians suddenly snatched the infant from his arms and ran away laughing.

The Indians became bolder as they watched more and more of the strange invaders dying. They began stealing anything they could take. They even climbed into the rigging of the anchored *San Carlos* and clipped out pieces of the sails. Then they attacked the weakened garrison. A Franciscan priest was wounded in the hand. One Spaniard was killed by an arrow through the throat. After driving the natives off by firing their muskets, the soldiers built a stockade around the tiny mission and didn't allow anyone to enter.

Their actions prevented further attacks. It also prevented Serra from making any converts. It was not a happy situation.

Meanwhile, Portolá and his men made their way slowly northward. Finally they reached the place where Monterey should have been. What they saw wasn't anything like Vizcaíno's glowing description. His extravagant praise had described a sheltered harbor that was protected from strong winds in any direction. What lay before them was simply a long curving bay. It was dangerously exposed, especially to north winds.

They headed farther north, with many men ill with scurvy. Soon they discovered the magnificent San Francisco Bay, which would prove to be far more important than Monterey in California's future development. But it wasn't what they were looking for. Even worse, the huge body of water reached so far inland that it blocked any further passage. With winter closing in and supplies running dangerously low, Portolá felt he

This illustration shows a priest demonstrating the Christian religion to a group of Indians. Generally these gatherings were peaceful. Occasionally, however, the Indians turned on the priests and some were killed.

had no choice but to return to San Diego. He arrived there in mid-January.

Serra had mixed feelings. On the one hand, he was delighted at Portolá's safe return. The soldiers also would provide further security from Indian attacks.

On the other hand, he was furious that Portolá hadn't found Monterey. Even though he had never seen it, Serra was convinced that it existed.

"You come from Rome without having seen the Pope," he snapped.

There was another concern. Portolá's return more than doubled the number of mouths to feed with steadily dwindling supplies. The *San José* had vanished without a trace, and there was still no sign of the *San Antonio*. Conditions grew steadily worse.

Portolá reached a decision: If no relief arrived by St. Joseph's Day, March 20, the entire expedition would have to abandon San Diego and return to its starting point in Baja California.

Serra was bitterly opposed to the move. He wrote, "There is even talk of abandonment and suppression of my poor little mission in San Diego. May God avert such a tragedy."

He had always lived his life according to the motto, "Always go forward, never go back."

For the first time he would have to "go back." He would have to abandon what he considered to be his life's work.

Portolá remained firm. If they ran out of food, he pointed out, they would all die.

On March 11, Serra began a novena, a nine-day prayer vigil. It would end the day before the deadline.

Each day when the prayers were over, some of the weary men clambered to the heights overlooking the ocean. There was nothing to see except the featureless procession of waves.■

An early map of Monterey Bay. If you rotate the book so that the lower left-hand corner of the illustration is pointing almost straight up, you will see its actual geographical position.

ON TO MONTEREY

On March 19, Serra and the other priests celebrated the final day of the novena with a feast. Again they made the climb.

A priest grabbed Serra's arm.

"Look, father!" the man exclaimed.

Far out to sea was the outline of a sail. It could only be the *San Antonio*, returning with reinforcements—and food.

While the men were disappointed when the ship continued on her way north and soon faded from sight, they rushed to Portolá with the exciting news. Seeing the ship on the final day of the novena seemed little short of miraculous.

Portolá decided to wait for the ship to come back.

Five days later what was indeed the *San Antonio* made her way into San Diego harbor. The men learned of what was deemed a second miracle. Believing that a settlement had already been established at Monterey, the *San Antonio* was headed there with her precious supplies. She had no intention of stopping at San Diego and had continued north. The captain decided to go ashore in the Santa Barbara channel. There, the local Indians told the crew that Portolá's expedition had returned two months previously.

The ship was loaded with food and supplies. There were also letters from Spanish authorities urging Portolá not to give up.

The Sacred Expedition had been saved.

A view of mission San Carlos Borroméo de Carmelo. Junípero Serra lived here for the final 14 years of his life. The statue at the right side of the picture is the same one that appears on page 22.

From then on, Father Serra celebrated a high mass on the 19th day of every month.

Portolá quickly reorganized the expedition. He would retrace his steps northward with about a dozen men. The *San Antonio* would take another group, which would include Serra. A handful would remain behind to guard San Diego.

The ship departed from San Diego on April 16, 1770. Portolá left the next day.

Traveling over a route that was now very familiar, Portolá made much better time. Just over a month later he and his men stood on the same shores that he'd visited the previous year. As they looked out over the calm water, they saw seals and spouting whales. They decided that they were finally at Vizcaíno's Monterey.

For Serra, the voyage wasn't quite as smooth. The winds blew mostly from the north, the very direction in which he wanted to sail.

"For days far from getting near to Monterey, we were getting farther and farther away from the goal of our desires," he wrote. "The result of it all was that the voyage lasted a full month and a half; and on May 31st, we entered and dropped anchor in the port—the object of so many controversies. We recognized it without any question, as being, both as to its underlying reality and its superficial landmarks, the same and unchanged spot where our ancestors the Spaniards landed."

On June 3, in front of an open-air altar, Father Serra conducted a formal mass. Soldiers happily firing their muskets and the deep boom of the *San Antonio's* cannons took the place of music. Serra blessed a large cross and sprinkled holy water on the earth around the men. He named the newly established mission San Carlos Borroméo de Carmelo.

When the religious rites were finished, Portolá performed a civic ceremony. He unfurled several royal flags and took possession of Monterey—as well as the other 150,000 square miles of Alta California—in the name of the Spanish king.

He had accomplished his mission. According to his orders, he named Lieutenant Pedro Fages to replace him as military governor and returned to Mexico City. When he arrived there, he received an enthusiastic welcome. He never returned to California.

But Serra's work had just begun.■

This illustration of Junípero Serra was made when he was an elderly man. It clearly shows the type of woolen robe that he wore for nearly his entire life. Compare this picture with the one on page 9.

ESTABLISHING THE MISSION SYSTEM

Monterey had been established. The soldiers built a small fort, called a presidio, to guard the new settlement.

Serra soon moved the mission several miles away from the presidio in search of better soil and a better water supply. Located near the present-day city of Carmel, San Carlos Borroméo would remain the focal point of the rest of his life.

He lived in a tiny room. A hard wooden cot was on one side. A trunk was on the other. Between them, next to the one window, was a small desk and chair. A single hook held his robe. A cross was mounted on the wall. That was all.

His duties as padre-president—responsible for the growth of the missions—required him to travel extensively. In 1771 he founded two more missions: San Antonio de Padua, about 50 miles south of San Carlos Borroméo, and San Gabriel Arcángel, east of present-day Los Angeles. The following year he established Mission San Luis Obispo, a little farther south of San Antonio de Padua.

These first missions, and the ones that would come after, followed a well-established pattern that Serra had first utilized in Sierra Gorda. In turn, that pattern rested on many decades of previous experience.

The first task was to select a good site for farming, with fertile soil and abundant water. Then a pueblo, or village, would be erected. There would also be a chapel for worship.

Normally a presidio would be nearby. It would contain a small garrison of soldiers, both to protect the pueblo from invaders and to impose discipline on the inhabitants.

Life on a mission quickly fell into a routine. The day would begin with a morning mass. Then everyone would eat hot corn mush for breakfast. At noon they would eat a stew made from corn and vegetables, with meat added on special occasions. Bread and corn mush were served at dinner. In addition, Father Serra and the other priests would spend several hours each day instructing the Indians about the Christian religion.

The success of the missions depended on having hundreds of Indians working in the fields to grow crops and taking care of the livestock. The farming way of life was completely different from what they were used to—hunting wild game and gathering forest plants. Some Indians willingly came to the missions. Others were either forced to come or were enticed with gifts such as glass beads or colored cloth.

The missionaries tried to baptize them as soon as possible. At that point they were called neophytes, from a Greek word that literally means "new plants." It was hoped that they would grow into a deeper knowledge of the Christian faith.

As neophytes, the Indians were under the authority of the missionaries. The position of the church was that spiritually the natives were to be treated like children. They couldn't leave the mission without permission and they would be punished for misbehaving.

Many of the Indians had difficulty adjusting to mission life. Living in one place was very different from the traveling way of life they had been accustomed to for many centuries. Unintentionally, the missionaries exposed them to diseases to which they had no immunity. Thousands would die over the next half century.

It was an isolated life for Serra and the other Franciscans. Many of the missions had only one or two priests. A supply ship came just once a year, carrying letters and other news of the outside world.

As the missions slowly began to prosper, Serra encountered problems with Fages, Portolá's successor as governor. For the most part, Serra and Portolá had gotten along well. Fages was another story.

Besides poor soil and lack of water, one of the reasons Serra had moved San Carlos Borroméo from its original site was problems with the soldiers under Fages's command. Most were unmarried, and sometimes they would attack the local Indian women. On other occasions soldiers would act brutally toward the Indians. It set a bad example when the friars preached a gospel of gentleness and love and their countrymen acted in the opposite manner.

Another problem was that there was some confusion as to who was actually in charge. Serra insisted that the mission Indians were under his control, but the soldiers often interfered with the way that he wanted to run the missions.

Fages began to complain that he didn't have enough men to adequately guard all of the new missions that Serra planned to establish.

In the autumn of 1772 Serra made the long, difficult journey to Mexico City to see the viceroy, or ruler, of New Spain. He made many suggestions to improve the operation of the missions. He also hoped that the viceroy would appoint a new military governor.

The viceroy was glad to hear firsthand news of California. Serra remained in Mexico City for seven months, finally leaving in August 1773. He returned to San Carlos Borroméo 10 months later, and soon had good news. Many of his proposals had been accepted, and Fages had been replaced.

The good news soured the following year. Because of a shortage of water, the original mission at San Diego had been moved inland, several miles from the presidio. The soldiers were no longer within a reasonable distance to protect it. After two Indians there were disciplined for theft, hundreds more attacked the mission, burned it to the ground, and killed several Spaniards. Among the dead was Fray Luis Jayme. He was also from Majorca, and Serra keenly felt his loss.

In 1776 two new missions were established. One was Mission Dolores in San Francisco, whose magnificent harbor the Spanish were just beginning to appreciate. The other was at San Juan Capistrano, about halfway between San Diego and modern-day Los Angeles. The church built there the following year still stands. It is the oldest Spanish building in California.

Mission Santa Clara de Asís, in what many people today call Silicon Valley because of the many computer companies that are located there, came the following year.

Serra would establish one more mission. It was San Buenaventura, founded in 1782 and now a parish church in the city of Ventura. He also selected the sites for a number of additional missions.

A picture of Mission San Juan Capistrano. Junípero Serra founded it in 1776, and the church which was built the following year is the oldest Spanish building in California.

By that point a primitive road known as El Camino Real—"the King's Highway," along virtually the same route as today's U.S. Highway 101—ran from San Diego to Monterey. Travelers on foot could look forward to sleeping every third night at a mission, which were 60 to 70 miles apart. Skilled riders could cover the distance in a single day.

The hardships of frontier life were taking their toll on Serra. From his point of view, Fages's successors turned out to be no improvement. He continued to disagree with all of them.

His leg and foot problems had become so severe that often he could barely walk. Even so, he continued to travel regularly among the missions, making most of his journeys on the back of mules. There is one record of his covering 70 miles on foot in two days. That would be difficult for a fit person today with well-supported hiking shoes, let alone a man in his 60s with a bad leg. A doctor on a ship that was visiting Monterey harbor at that time offered to treat it, but Serra said that he was too busy.

In addition to his constant leg pain, his habit of beating himself on the chest with a large stone while preaching may have damaged his rib cage.

Late in 1783 he wrote to one of the Franciscans, "The nearness of my own death is constantly before me; more especially as I feel I am breaking up in health."

He had enough energy to make one final visit to all the missions in the first part of 1784, but by August he sensed that the end was near. He sent for Father Palóu.

"He is nearly finished," a soldier told the priest.

On the night of August 27, he took his final communion.

He felt slightly better the following morning. Father Palóu sprinkled his room with holy water and read the Commendation for a Departing Soul. Serra lay down to rest and Father Palóu left to get some broth.

When he returned, Serra had died, most likely of a heart attack.

He was buried the following day near the church altar at his beloved San Carlos Borroméo. The funeral ceremonies included a requiem mass, the firing of cannons from ships anchored offshore, and officials carrying the coffin around the mission grounds.

"Perhaps more impressive was the tribute from the natives, whom Junípero loved so much and served so well," writes M.N.L. Couve de Murville in his book *The Man Who Founded California*. "Their crying and wailing almost drowned the singing of the Office of the Dead. Palóu is surely right in commenting: 'The sons were lamenting the death of their father who, having left his own aging parents in his homeland, had come to this distant place for the sole purpose of making them his spiritual children.' This was Junípero Serra's finest epitaph." ∎

Father Fermin Francisco de Lasuen became Father-President of the California missions in 1785, not long after Serra's death. Born in 1736, he arrived in Mexico in 1761 and joined the San Diego mission in 1773. After moving several times, he returned to San Diego in 1777 to become the mission's leader. He held the position until 1785 when he moved to Mission San Carlos Borroméo as Serra's successor. Under his leadership, nine more missions were established and many of the older ones were expanded. He died in 1803.

SAINT JUNIPERO SERRA?

CHAPTER 8

After Serra's death, Father Palóu briefly became head of the California missions. He was soon replaced by Father Fermín Francisco de Lasuén, who was responsible for designing the beautiful churches that came to symbolize the missions. He founded nine more before his death in 1803. Another three were added during the next 20 years.

The 21 missions soon became very prosperous, and that prosperity made many other settlers jealous. They resented all the land and livestock that the missions controlled. When Mexico revolted and became independent from Spain in 1821, the new government began to reduce the influence of the missions. The missionaries were replaced by secular priests who did not try to convert people. Many mission lands were taken away and made into vast ranchos under private ownership.

Less than three decades later, California was given to the young United States at the conclusion of the Mexican-American War. Within two years it became the 31st state in the Union. The new state government had no interest in the missions. Eventually most were entirely deserted.

By the 1880s most of the mission sites and their buildings were in a state of serious decay. A tourist during that period wrote that she doubted if there was anywhere on earth that was "colder, barer, uglier or dirtier" than a California mission.

Soon afterward a combination of groups including the Landmarks Club, businesspeople, and state government officials worked to restore the missions. It took many years, but today thousands of visitors every year walk through the gardens and graceful buildings that owe their origins to Serra's energy and dedication.

His legacy lives on in other ways. He is often referred to as the Father of California, with a double meaning: both as the primary Catholic Father and also as the man who brought California into being. Schools, libraries, museums, mountain peaks, and parks are named for him. Even part of a freeway in San Mateo County bears his name—though it's hard to believe that he would approve of the frantic, fast-paced driving that takes place there. His statues appear in many places around the state.

A nearly nine-foot-high bronze statue of Junípero Serra stands in the National Statuary Hall Collection in the U.S. Capitol in Washington, D.C. Each of the 50 states is allowed to honor two people who were vitally important in its founding and development. Serra was one of California's choices. His statue, the work of Italian sculptor Ettore Cadorin, was erected in 1931. Serra cradles the model of a mission church in his left hand as he gazes up at the cross held high in his right hand.

In 1963, the 250th anniversary of Serra's birth, an act of Congress authorized the coining of a special national medal containing his likeness. He was the first Catholic priest to receive such an honor.

In 1934, one hundred and fifty years after his death, a movement to make him a saint in the Catholic Church began. In the nearly 2,000-year history of the church, only about 1,000 people have been canonized, or elevated to the status of sainthood.

Canonization is a long, very complicated process that involves three stages: Venerable, Blessed, and Saint.

The first step for Serra came in 1985. After more than 50 years of research and thousands of written documents established Serra's virtuousness and piety, Pope John Paul II named him "Venerable."

To become "Blessed" requires proof of at least one miracle that can be directly traced to the person under consideration for sainthood. Most miracles are of a medical nature and require intensive investigation to be sure that there is no scientific explanation.

In 1960 an Illinois nun named Sister Mary Boniface Dyrda was about to die of a disease known as systemic lupus erythematosus. She received the last rites. A Franciscan chaplain offered a novena to Serra. Almost immediately the sister made a rapid recovery. When her physicians could offer no medical explanation for her sudden cure, the Church accepted it as a miracle. Pope John Paul II, who had praised Serra during a visit to

This statue of Junípero Serra stands in the graveyard at Mission Dolores in San Francisco. Portolá discovered San Francisco Bay in 1770, and Serra founded the mission there six years later. Today San Francisco is one of California's most important cities.

San Carlos Borroméo de Carmelo in 1987, beatified him—made him Blessed—the following year.

At that point a controversy began that continues to this day.

Father Serra's many admirers were understandably pleased. They felt that his life reflected a truly extraordinary degree of faith and holiness.

But those who criticized the mission movement, including some Native American groups, opposed his canonization. Some called him a sadist. Other terms such as *sinner, fanatic,* and *enslaver* were used to describe him.

A few went even further, suggesting that what he did was similar to the Holocaust against the Jews by Nazi Germany during World War II.

The summer 1989 issue of the *Journal of San Diego History* contains a review of a book entitled *The Missions of California: A Legacy of Genocide.*

According to the book, the review explains, "The arrival of the Europeans was a cultural and demographic catastrophe for the California Indians. Too often it is forgotten that Serra aimed not just to convert the Indians to Catholicism but to eradicate Indian culture as well. It is in this sense that the book's subtitle, *A Legacy of Genocide,* is justified. Many of Serra's fiercest critics are individuals actively engaged in efforts to heal Indian society by recovering and honoring the traditional ways that bound tribes together for centuries. The attempt to sanctify a man who dedicated his life to the destruction of those ways is, understandably, galling to them."

Serra's supporters reply that there is no evidence that he personally mistreated any Indians. On the contrary, they say, he often tried to intervene when soldiers and civil authorities dealt brutally with them.

They add that Catholic missionaries during Serra's era had a set of beliefs about non-Christian peoples that no longer exists. The Second Vatican Council recognized that native cultures contain many elements that need to be maintained. Missionaries today must recognize that "whatever goodness is found in the minds and hearts of men, or in the particular customs and cultures of peoples, far from being lost is purified, raised to a higher level and reaches its perfection," according to the 1965 Decree on the Church's Missionary Activity, *Ad Gentes Divinitus.*

Therefore those criticisms didn't stop the efforts to canonize Father Serra.

Sainthood, the third and final level, is a carefully regulated process. It combines church law several centuries old with the most modern medical technologies. Under a recent ruling, only miraculous events occurring after a person has been beatified can be considered. That limits Serra's supporters to events occurring after 1987. Even with this limitation, at one point more than 20 different events were being considered. The ones that are believed to present the strongest evidence of the direct intercession of Serra with God will be submitted as the final stage of his canonization.

If Serra does become a saint, his life and beliefs officially become models to be emulated by other Catholics.

Certainly anyone could admire the strength of his faith that drove him to travel countless miles under the most primitive conditions despite a constantly sore leg. His selfless devotion to his beliefs is also admirable.

As Father Palóu wrote in his biography of Serra, which was published in 1787, "His memory shall not fail, because the works he performed when alive shall be impressed in the minds of the dwellers of this New California; despite the ravages of time, they shall not be forgotten." ■

CHRONOLOGY

1713   born on November 24 in the Majorcan village of Petra

1729   at Majorca's capital city of Palma, begins studies to enter priest-hood

1730   begins novitiate in Franciscan order

1731   takes vows as Franciscan friar

1737   begins teaching in Franciscan friary

1742   receives doctorate in theology and is appointed professor at University of Palma

1749   volunteers to travel to New Spain as missionary

1750   walks from Veracruz on Mexico coast to Mexico City, then becomes missionary in Sierra Gorda

1758   returns to San Fernando and conducts "home missions"

1767   is appointed head of missions in Baja California

1768   is appointed to found missions in Alta California as part of Sacred Expedition

1769   arrives in San Diego and founds San Diego de Alcalá, the first mission in California

1770   arrives in Monterey and founds Mission San Carlos Borroméo de Carmelo

1771   founds Missions San Antonio de Padua and San Gabriel Arcángel

1772   founds Mission San Luis Obispo de Tolosa; travels to Mexico City to meet with the viceroy of New Spain

1776   founds Missions San Francisco de Asís and San Juan Capistrano

1777   founds Mission Santa Clara de Asís

1782   founds Mission San Buenaventura

1784   dies on August 28

TIMELINE

1181   St. Francis of Assisi is born

1209   Franciscan order is founded

1492   Christopher Columbus discovers New World

1513   Vasco Núñez de Balboa becomes first European to see Pacific Ocean

1521   Hernán Cortés conquers Mexico

1536   Cortés establishes colony in lower California and gives the land its name

1542   Juan Rodríguez Cabrillo sails up California coast to Oregon border and claims land for Spain

1602   Sebastián Vizcaíno surveys West Coast and discovers Monterey

1607   English settlers found Jamestown Colony on Chesapeake Bay

1620   Pilgrims land in Massachusetts and establish Plymouth Bay Colony

1697   Jesuits found mission at Loreto in Baja California, first permanent settlement in the Californias

1701–1702   Jesuit Father Eusebio Kino proves that California is not an island

1767   Captain Gaspar de Portolá becomes Governor of Baja California; King Carlos III banishes Jesuits from New Spain and the Franciscans take over the missions

1769   Sacred Expedition arrives in San Diego

1770   On second attempt, Portolá discovers Monterey, where Father Junípero Serra establishes Mission San Carlos Borroméo de Carmelo

1774   Juan Bautista de Anza opens land route from Mexico to California

1776   Thirteen English colonies sign Declaration of Independence from Great Britain

1821   Mexico wins independence from Spain

1848   California is given to the United States after Mexican-American War

1850   California is admitted to United States as 31st state

FURTHER READING

For Young Adults:

Behrens, June. *Missions of the Central Coast*. Minneapolis: Lerner Publications, 1996.

Dolan, Sean. *Junípero Serra: Spanish Missionary and Explorer*. Minneapolis: Econo-Clad Books, 1999.

Genet, Donna. *Father Junípero Serra: Founder of California Missions*. Berkeley Heights, N.J.: Enslow Publishers, 1996.

Morgado, Martin. Junípero Serra: *A Pictorial Biography*. Monterey, Calif.: Siempre Adelante Publishing, 1991.

Rawls, James. *Never Turn Back: Father Serra's Mission*. New York: Raintree/Steck-Vaughn, 1996.

Works Consulted:

Ainsworth, Katherine, and Ed Ainsworth. *In the Shade of the Juniper Tree: A Life of Fray Junípero Serra*. Garden City, N.Y.: Doubleday and Company, 1970.

Bean, Walton, and James Rawls. *California: An Interpretive History*. New York: McGraw-Hill, 1988.

Couve de Murville, M.N.L. *The Man Who Founded California: The Life of Blessed Junípero Serra*. San Francisco: Ignatius Press, 2000.

Lyngheim, Linda. *Father Junípero Serra: The Traveling Missionary*. Van Nuys, Calif.: Langtry Publications, 1986.

Palóu, Francisco. *Palou's Life of Fray Junípero Serra*. Translated and annotated by Maynard J. Geiger, O.F.M. Washington, D.C.: Academy of American Franciscan History, 1955.

Riesenberg, Felix, Jr. *The Golden Road: The Story of California's Mission Trail*. New York: McGraw-Hill, 1962.

ON THE WEB

California Mission Studies Association
www.ca-missions.org

The California Mission Site
www.californiamissions.com

San Carlos Borroméo de Carmelo Mission
www.carmelmission.org

San Diego Historical Society
www.sandiegohistory.org

Serra's San Diego
www.sandiegohistory.org/books/ssd/ssd.htm

The Path to Glory
www.serraus.org/news_&_events/the_serran/the_serran_mar01/
v55_3Mar01p4.htm

GLOSSARY

adobe (ah-DOE-bee)—a type of clay; mixed with straw and water, it is used to form bricks

canonization (can-un-eye-ZAY-shun)—the process by which someone becomes a saint in the Catholic Church

conquistador (con-KEE-stah-door)—any of the 16th-century Spanish soldiers who explored and conquered territory in the New World

emulate (EM-you-late)—to imitate an admired person in an effort to become like him or her

epitaph (EH-peh-taff)—an inscription or monument honoring a person who has died

Franciscan (fran-SIS-can)—a member of Orders of Friars Minor, founded by St. Francis of Assisi in 1209 and dedicated to charity and missionary work friar (FRY-er)—a member of a Roman Catholic order

friary (FRY-er-ee)—the residence or community of persons under religious vows

genocide (JEN-oh-side)—intentionally killing an entire race, religion, or other group of people

habit—distinctive style of clothing

immunity (im-MYOO-nih-tee)—biological protection against a disease

Jesuit (JES-oo-it)—a member of a Catholic religious order known as the Society of Jesus. It was founded by St. Ignatius Loyola in 1540 and became very powerful over the following two centuries

mission—a church or settlement area established by religious leaders to spread their beliefs to other people

missionary—a person who goes among different peoples to teach the beliefs of his or her religion

muleteer (MYOOL-teer)—a person who drives and cares for mules

neophyte (NEE-oh-fite)—someone who has just converted to a new religion, such as a New World Indian who has become a member of a Catholic community

novice (NAH-viss)—a person who has recently entered a religious order but has not yet taken vows

novitiate (no-VIH-shee-it)—a period of time served by a novice before he or she can take religious vows

penance (PEN-ence)—voluntary punishment to achieve forgiveness of sins

poultice (POLE-tiss)—a moist, soft healing substance applied to an inflamed part of the body to provide relief

presidio (preh-SEE-dee-oh)—Spanish fort used to protect nearby areas

pueblo (PWEH-blow)—an Indian village

sadist (SADE-ist)—one who enjoys inflicting pain on others

secular (SEK-you-lur)—not specifically religious

viceroy (VICE-roy)—a governor in a country ruled by a king or other sovereign

INDEX

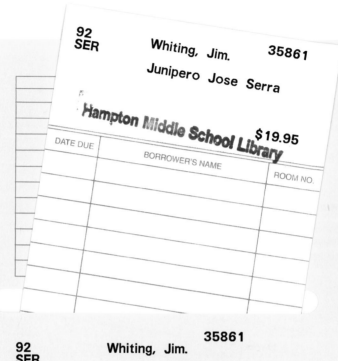

92
SER

Whiting, Jim.   **35861**

Junipero Jose Serra